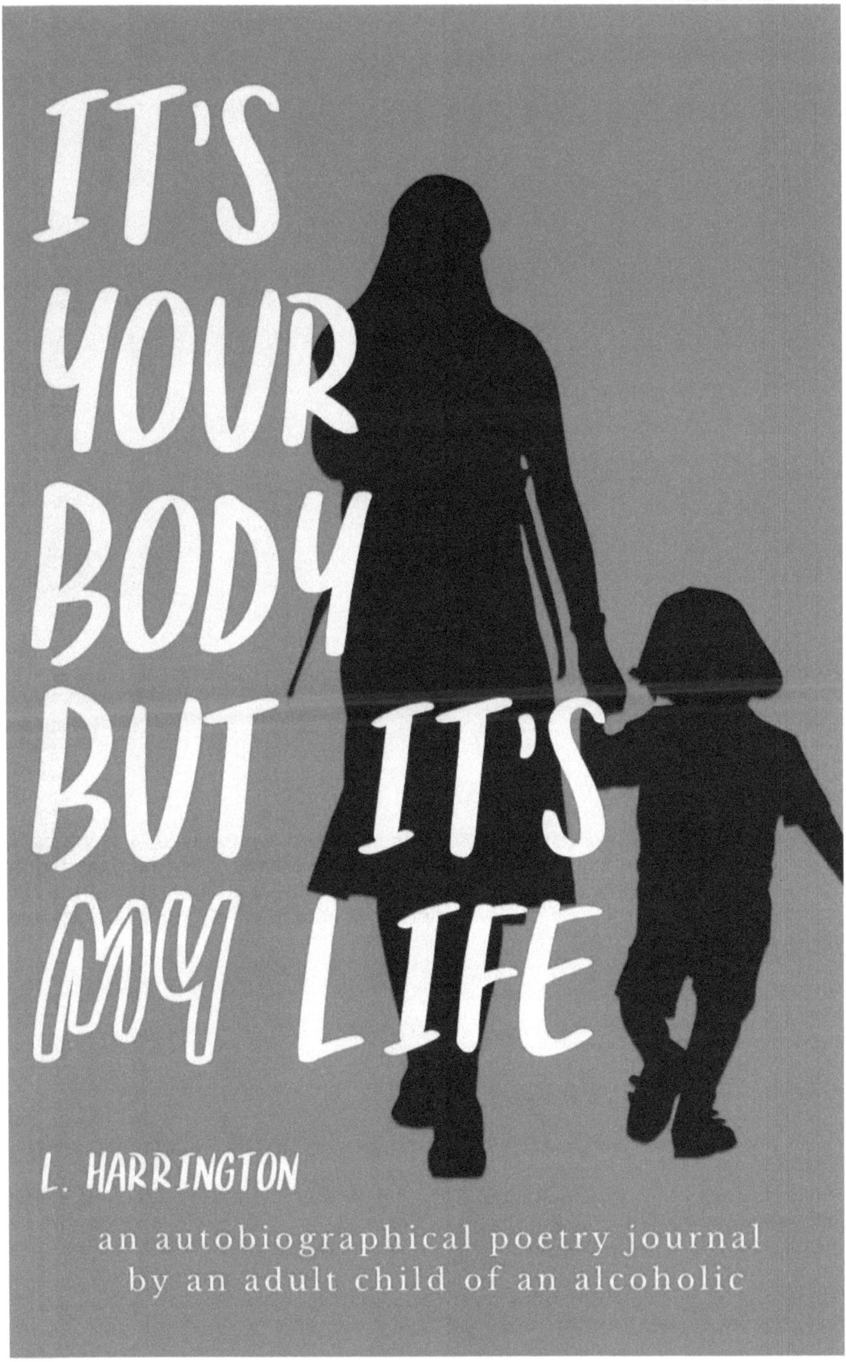

IT'S YOUR BODY BUT IT'S MY LIFE

L. HARRINGTON

an autobiographical poetry journal
by an adult child of an alcoholic

ISBN Paperback: 978-1-954493-84-1

Published by Green Heart Living Press

Cover Design by Elizabeth B. Hill

Cover Image Credit: "Mother and Child Illustration" by mskathrynne from pixabay

This is a work of creative nonfiction. The events are portrayed to the best of the author's memory. While all the stories in this book are true, names and identifying details have been changed to protect the privacy of the people involved.

Any errors or misrepresentations regarding Internal Family Systems (IFS), therapy terminology, etc. are the sole responsibility of the author.

Dedication

Contents

Prologue

L. Harrington is not my name. Since I am an adult child of an alcoholic, and grew up surrounded by lies, I want to start with the truth so you will recognize the truth throughout this book. I am using a pseudonym because some of the thoughts, reflections and feelings written here reflect the thoughts and feelings of what it was like to experience these things at age 10, from the perspective of a 10-year-old. As an adult, I fully understand the stress that was upon my extended family, due to the lifestyle choices of my mother. I realize how blessed we were to have family step up, step in, and take us into their homes. As a child, however, I did not fully grasp that, and I don't want my 10-year-old self's feelings to taint the lives and memories of those who rescued us. I hope you can understand my decision.

Autobiographies typically get into the details of when and where everyone was born, where they lived, went to school, worked, etc. However, this is not so much an autobiography of the physical being, but of the emotional being. And since the poetry is mostly about identifying feelings, and feelings transcend timelines, I have skipped most of the dates and locations pertaining to my life. Instead, I will tell you the things I think you'd want to know.

My parents met and married in Connecticut, where my mom had spent most of her life. She was 17 when they met and 18 when they married. She was employed, but did not have a high school diploma. My dad was an engineer from Wisconsin, where he had lived until relocating to Connecticut for his job. He had a master's degree and was 24 when he married my mom. His job required a lot of traveling, so they were not in Connecticut for long. Eventually they had three children (the youngest being me), each born in a different state, due to dad's job relocations.

Between the traveling, new homes, new towns, new friends and the distance from her family, my mom's mental health took a turn for the worse. She experienced anxiety and nervousness. On top of that, my dad's job required a lot of mingling, and so eventually the occasional drink for my mom turned into a regular routine—and then some.

About a month before I turned two, my dad had a stroke that left him incapacitated and institutionalized until his death 15 years later. My mom suddenly found herself half a continent away from her family, with an almost 2-year-old, an 8-year-old, an 11-year-old, and few job skills. While my dad's mom attempted to assist, it was too much. So about eight months after dad's stroke, we (me, my mom, and my siblings) left Wisconsin and returned to Connecticut to be closer to mom's family.

We moved into a project where we stayed for a few years. While I don't have many recollections of living there, as I was young, I do remember that I loved it. There were many families there, a lot of children, and a large field where we could run and play. I had freedom to roam—partly because I stayed out of trouble and partly because my mom rarely cared or knew of my whereabouts—even at the young ages of five and six.

At some point we moved about a mile away into an apartment in a three-family home. Although my school system stayed the same, I missed the constant companionship of children in the project. We were now on a busier street, and an "older" area, and there were not a lot of children my age. Also, since we were in a busier area, I had lost the freedom—and the field—I had to roam around.

Moving is traumatic for children. Adults like to quip that "children are resilient," but saying it does not make it true. I had no warning of the move, of the loss of friendships, and of a familiar environment. This was an isolating time for me. My sister and brother were now old enough to be out on dates, hang around with friends, and/or had jobs to go to, so more often than not, I was home alone with Mom and I had lost my "escape"—my playtime and friends. As for mom, she didn't skip a beat. Her drinking chair made the move with us, so she still had her best friend by her side, so to speak.

Back in the day, there was very little being done regarding mental health and alcoholism, so Mom basically went untreated. Every so often she would be admitted to Norwich State Hospital to "dry-out." Norwich State Hospital was a psychiatric hospital but served as a catch-all for people who had no other recourse. To our knowledge, there was no actual treatment going on for mom's alcoholism, just a place that was liquor-free to allow her to dry-out. These stints lasted for three to four months at a time, and during those times we were blessed to have aunts and uncles who would take us in.

One Easter Sunday, things took a permanent turn. Even as a child, I knew this was it. My sister and I arrived home from church and the house was a mess. We located mom in a heap on the floor and immediately called the aunts. I have no recollection of whether my sister then called for an ambulance or if we waited for the aunts to arrive and then they made the decision to call the ambulance. I remember the aunts arriving and a few had brought their children with them. I was banished to the driveway in the backyard with my cousins, most likely so all of us would avoid the trauma of seeing the ambulance remove my mom. We stood in that driveway in silence, all of us too young to find the right words ... if such a thing even exists in this circumstance. I have no recall of the rest of that day. I don't know if the aunts and cousins left and we cleaned up the apartment and tried to adjust to our new normal; or if we went with one of them to their house to celebrate Easter and then someone drove us back home. Those memories are locked away somewhere.

As my brother was legally an adult at that point in time, a decision was made for the three of us to stay in the apartment so that my sister and I could finish out the school year in our existing schools. Mom was sent someplace to dry out—it may have been Norwich State Hospital again—and then eventually went to what would now be called an assisted living facility. She would remain there until her death, 15 years later.

When the school year came to a close, my brother got an apartment with a friend. He commuted to college and worked part-time. My sister had to complete her last year of high school, so she went to live with one aunt and uncle for about 18 months, until she got her high school diploma and a job and moved into an apartment with a friend. I went to a different aunt and uncle for two years. At the close of those two years, my brother (being nine years older) got married and then he and his new wife took me in to live with them. I was just starting eighth grade and I lived with them until about nine months after I graduated college.

A couple of years ago, my brother died. But he was so much more than my brother. When our dad had gotten sick, he had told our great aunt, "I am the only father she will ever know." So, he was a dad, friend, mentor, and brother to me. As a child, he was the one I went to when I was afraid at night. He was the one who sparked my interest in music. I would sit in his room with him and listen to songs of Simon and Garfunkel; Crosby, Stills, Nash and Young; John Denver; and Jim Croce. He loved learning and playing new games and card games, and I was quickly hooked on that, too. In short, most of what he loved, I loved.

Upon his death I learned that I was the executrix of his estate and, as is probably typical of an adult child of an alcoholic, I went right into business mode, skipping over the grieving mode because, who needs to waste time on that? Within four months of my brother passing, my body started to give way. Sleeplessness; severe reflux; sadness; acne; blood pressure issues. I went to my P.A. (Physician's Assistant) to get a pill, because, certainly that would take care of all of my problems. Wouldn't it?

I am one of the lucky ones. I had a P.A. who asked if something had changed recently and so I mentioned that my brother had died and I was under some stress from that, but "I could handle it." I just needed something to make the reflux go away which would help me be able to sleep. As an afterthought I said, "I probably should see someone."

And here is what changed everything. She could have said, "Yes that is a good idea." She could have just written a script and sent me on my way. But she didn't just hear me, she listened to me. She said, "Wait one minute," and left the room. When she returned, she had a name and a phone number written down for me. She handed it to me and said, "I've heard people have good results with this person, you may want to reach out to this therapist."

We talked a bit more and then yes, she gave me a script, too. But here's the thing: Because she made the effort to give me the name and phone number of a therapist, I felt indebted to at least call the number, whereas I would have waited another several months to investigate therapists on my own before finally (hopefully) reaching out to one. I ended up dialing the number that day, after I picked up the script. I got an answering machine, and almost hung up, but again, I felt indebted, so I left my name and number. Receiving that phone number saved my life.

When the therapist returned my call, I mentioned my brother had died and that I just needed to meet one or two times "to set myself straight." I'm pretty sure I could hear the smile in the therapist's voice when the therapist repeated, "Just one or two sessions, huh?" We set a date. Over a year later, we still met weekly. My therapist was my second lifesaver.

During my lifetime, I had seen two or three other therapists. My first two exposures to therapy were with a marriage counselor, as my husband and I needed help getting through some rough patches. My third exposure to therapy was when I was "bumped" from an employment position with no warning. I was not given any time to say goodbye to those coworkers who I treasured. Shortly thereafter I was assigned to a new position but found myself struggling to adjust. I could not identify my feelings—they were all over the place. I took advantage of the Employee Assistance Program and went to a therapist. She gave a name to the hodge-podge of feelings: grief. And she was right. After a couple of sessions with her, I felt I had the tools I needed to adjust, and I ended up settling in and loving the new position.

When my brother died, I recognized the hodge-podge of feelings as grief, but didn't know what to do with all of them. I had always been great at compartmentalizing my feelings, but this time around, my body would have none of that. In therapy I was introduced to grief recovery. After working on grief recovery for my brother, I moved on to my mom, my dad, and others, both living and dead. I learned so much about grief and feelings, that I didn't want to stop there. And so, we moved on to discuss and to uncover and to feel the childhood trauma of my dad getting sick, mom's alcoholism, abandonment, and me and my siblings living on and off with aunts and uncles for months at a time when mom was "drying out."

Somewhere around the six-month point, I was introduced to the concept of the "Empty Chair." In this exercise, you sit across from an empty chair and envision a part of yourself (say, a younger version of yourself), or another person sitting across from you, then ask questions and formulate answers to uncover feelings or discover where attitudes and behaviors may originate. We had been talking about a childhood trauma I had experienced when I was around 10, a few months after the Easter Day episode. The aunts and uncles had come over to discern which of us would go where. The car ride to the aunt and uncle's house I was to live with was intimidating to a 10-year-old. In working to help me process the trauma of the car ride to my aunt and uncle's house, one day my therapist said, "Let's give the Empty Chair concept a try," and then repositioned an empty chair to face me, head on. When that chair was shifted, my universe shifted with it. It was the first time I experienced dissociation and, with it, PTSD from the night of the car ride. It was terrifying. It was horrible. It was unexpected. I had no idea I had that much fear residing in me; as an adult I was overwhelmed by it. It gave me a new appreciation for my young self and what I had survived.

As a 12-year-old, I had read the wonderful book, *Up a Road Slowly* by Irene Hunt, and I remember relating to Julie's life and thoughts and feelings—that they mirrored mine in some ways. And I thought, *someday I am going to write a book about my experiences.* Over the decades, I attempted to do this several times, to no avail. After the Empty Chair exercise, when I was finally able and willing to *feel* the pain of those memories rather than just wanting to write about memories, the words came rushing forward, but as poetry, not prose.

This autobiographical poetry journal is my story from the time I recognized something was going on with my mom—a dawn of consciousness of her drinking, so to speak—until current day. The poems that follow are autobiographical in nature and are based on my memories of growing up. They are not a day-by-day accounting of my life. For almost all of them, I journaled about events or locations to provide background. For those who have lived through alcoholism or addiction, no background information is needed to explain the feelings. We have all been there, in one form or another. If you have never been able to put words to some of your thoughts, feelings or pain, I hope you find them here.

My therapy journey continues to this day. If you are struggling, I encourage you to search for a wonderful, compassionate, caring therapist to join you on your journey, even if only for a bit. Compassion is an amazingly powerful tool. It is powerful when you are on the giving side of it, the receiving side of it, and when you have the grace to bestow it upon yourself. I hope you find a therapist who envelops you in compassion.

When I First Had a Clue

When I was four and we were living in the project, I remember my mother sitting at the kitchen table, smoking a cigarette with a drink by her side, gazing off into the distance. I had a pad and pencil, and I was doodling things, trying to write the alphabet, and asking her to look, and did I get it right? She barely acknowledged me, so I eventually left the room. A year or so after that, when we had moved to a three-family house, I was a little older and wiser. While I still didn't know exactly what was going on, I knew something was not right.

When I First Had a Clue

Do you remember the day I first had a clue
About what was in your glass?
I do. It was quite a breakthrough.

I got thirsty, and I saw your glass next to you.
Why get my own drink, I thought,
I only want a sip or two.

Half the time, you were asleep in that stupid chair.
But when your liquor's involved,
You become alert and aware.

Before I realized it, you slapped my hand—hard.
I withdrew it quickly,
Realizing I'd let down my guard.

"Don't touch that. Go get your own," you thickly barked at me.
I backed up, holding in tears,
Not expecting an apology.

But thank you for that lesson, because then I knew
It wasn't water in there,
But something else that made you not you.

It's Your Body But It's MY Life

I imagine that anyone who is a child of an alcoholic hates the following statement as much as I do:

"I can do what I want. It's my body."

I always want to respond, "Yes, it's *your* body. But it's MY life that gets caught up in the trail of destruction that you leave behind."

It's Your Body, But It's MY Life

It's your body,
But it's MY life,
And each drink you drink is like a knife that removes
My sense of control, My sense of self.
The laughter and joy from within our house.

The booze you buy
Each drink you pour
Erodes my self-confidence a little more.
My courage, my compassion, and my calm,
My curiosity and independence—all gone.

Replaced with fear.
Replaced with shame.
Replaced with happenings that I can't name
Or share or tell. You have taught me well.
SILENCE is the name of this game.

The Shape Shifter

I still remember the day I found my mother's hiding place for her liquor—it was under the kitchen sink. I promptly took the bottle and unscrewed the cap, preparing to empty the contents down the drain. My sister walked into the kitchen and warned, "Don't do it. She'll kill you. Don't do it." Hearing the fear in her voice put some fear into me, so I emptied only half of the contents. "She'll never notice," I quipped. "She never notices anything."

But she DID notice.

When something is a priority to you, you pay attention.

Note on the following poem: In the 1960s, a child could go to a store with a signed note and money to buy cigarettes for an adult.

The Shape Shifter

Your excuse is "It's my body,"
As you down another drink.
"I'm not hurting anyone,"
Is what you like to think.

But I am the shape shifter
And I follow you around,
I become your caretaker
As I lift you from the ground.

And sometimes I am your gopher
As you send me to the store
To get cigarettes for you,
"And don't dare get anything more!"

Another day I'm your groomer,
Since you can't get dressed alone.
Also, I'm a secretary,
I fetch mail and answer the phone.

Mainly I'm the housemaid,
Stripping your sheets, which are urine-soaked.
Making the bed the best I can.
This day's not going as I hoped.

You know the level of your liquor,
You know how to mix a drink,
But you don't know where I am,
What I like, or what I think.

I don't think about tomorrow,
It will crush me with its weight.
I'm just living day-to-day,
And pretty soon I will turn eight.

The Bathtub Prayer

When you are a child, and you are put into the position of having to be the adult, it is brutal. You do not have the knowledge, reasoning power, or strength of an adult. But as a child, you don't realize this. All you know is that you either succeeded or failed at what you were expected to do. And for me, each failure hammered home the negative messages.

The Bathtub Prayer

I don't remember how old I was
The first time I had to get you off the floor.
I do remember you'd fallen in the bathroom
And I had problems opening the door.

Every time I would attempt to lift you
You'd slur, "I'm sorry," and collapse back down.
I was running out of courage and strength
And sat on the bathtub and looked around.

"I need help, I can't do this alone," I prayed.
And got to my feet to try yet again.
But my prayer was answered—I lifted you up—
So this time you would walk, not crawl, then.

But why should a child have to lift an adult?
And each time we can't, what message is received?
"I am weak. I'm inept. I'm incompetent,"
Are some of the messages I misconceived.

I know. It's *your* body. But you need to know
That your choices are taking a toll on *ME*.
Will I ever have confidence in my Self
When I'm failing these tasks so frequently?

Courage in the Face of Fear

Perspective is an important tool.

So many times, when I look back at my inability to lift my mother, I associate it with negative traits, like weakness or incompetence. But taking a different perspective, I can look back and realize that, no matter how afraid I was each time I heard that sound, I always responded.

Courage in the Face of Fear

I hear the thud, and want to pretend I don't.
I hope you'll lift yourself, but I know you won't.

I turn up the volume so that I won't hear,
And then curl into a ball, a ball of fear.

A ball of failure, exhaustion, weakness, shame;
As I wonder how much longer we'll play this game.

I want to quit. I'm not equipped for all this.
I want a normal childhood to reminisce.

But no one else is around—it's just us two.
So, I uncurl, and head in to try to lift you.

I'm Sorry ... Yet Again

My mom was not a mean drunk. My sister and I would sometimes count our blessings about that fact. (My brother would never discuss "the situation." Not when we were younger, and not when we were adults.) Mom didn't yell, scream, or belittle. On the flip side, neither did she talk to us, console us, or praise us. But one thing she consistently *did* do was to constantly say, "I'm sorry." I grew to hate those words. The insincerity of them. Or at least I judged them to be insincere, since nothing ever changed. I was still left to struggle with the chaos, trying to keep my head above water. As an adult, I used to wonder why I found it so difficult to say, "I'm sorry," until I wrote this poem.

I'm Sorry ... Yet Again

If someone says "I'm sorry"
But never changes how they act, what they say or what they do,
It means nothing to me.
Does it mean something to you?

You say "I'm sorry" all day:
When you realize we saw you pour the last drink you took;
When you fall to the floor;
When you are too drunk to cook.

You are sorry at bedtime,
When I wonder if things will change, and when—or if I will care.
Or will I already
Be drinking from my own chair?

You say "I'm sorry" each hour
And I beg God's forgiveness when you say it every day,
But you need to know "I'm sorry"
Doesn't take the hate away.

I hated being the adult,
Feeling inept, struggling to do things I shouldn't have to do yet.
Always being sorry sounds great,
But does it repay your debt?

I wish I knew the answer.
I wish I could let bygones be bygones, forgive and forget.
But mainly, I wish I could
Live without all this regret.

The Slap

Generally, mom was "out of it" by early afternoon. This particular day was seemingly no different, so when I heard the knock on the door, I got up to answer it. I had answered the door before, without consequences, so I am at a loss as to why it was unacceptable on this day. But then, that is part of the problem, isn't it? Children of alcoholics always need to be on guard because the rules are constantly changing. I was on high alert for weeks after that, wondering if a new pattern had been established. But my brother's warning was heard, and my mother never physically harmed me again.

The Slap

There was a knock at the door,
So I got up from the floor
Where I was playing with the cat.

You were sitting in your chair—
In the usual place where
You sit and polish off your drinks.

I opened the door—it was Jim.
Were you too drunk to recognize him?
Maybe, since you leapt from the chair

And slapped me—hard—in the face.
Before I registered the disgrace
Of it, Jim promptly slapped you back.

"Don't ever touch her again!"
He yelled, and that was when
We all began to cry.

I cried for me—that slap hurt.
And now I'd need to be alert
To more than just your aloofness.

I shed tears for my brother,
Himself a child, with no other
Choice but to quickly become a man.

His childhood got left behind,
And now he was being defined
By his reactions to things that you do.

I didn't have tears for you.
Just anger and shame, which grew
As you said, yet again, "I'm sorry."

I wondered if Jim cried
Because he was beside
Himself at the reversal of these roles.

And as for you, why those tears?
Did you finally realize the weight he bears,
While you stand on the sidelines of your life?

Guarded

Looking back, I did not ever sense or recognize that I was becoming guarded. I think it must have occurred in increments. Being attentive turned into being watchful which morphed into alertness which progressed to protectiveness which cemented into guarded.

Guarded

I've been told I'm "guarded,"
And I suppose that is true.
You quickly learn to be on guard
When no one is protecting you.

When your mom is aloof,
And doesn't care where you are,
You are guarded against others
So you observe them from afar.

When you're slapped in the face
Just for opening the door,
You're guarded against punishments
You never worried about before.

When moving is the norm,
And you don't know where or when,
You're guarded about getting close—
About making new friends ... again.

When you're told your body
Is curved in the wrong places,
You're guarded against what thoughts lurk
Behind other people's faces.

When you've learned it's yourself
You should rely on each day,
You are guarded about trusting—
It's easier to stay away.

When you feel unwelcome,
But there's no place else to go,
You're guarded about loving Self—
And you diminish, blow-by-blow.

Guarded is who I am.
Guarded is all that I know.
Guarded's become my default mode.
I'm not sure I can let it go.

Mealtimes

At a family gathering with my adult children, my sister, and her adult children, we were all talking about favorite and least favorite meals. My sister brought up memories of TV dinners of Salisbury steak. That was the first time any of the kids had heard of TV dinners and Salisbury steak and they were intrigued, though not for long. That led to stories of the chop suey and noodles, which garnered laughter. I never ventured into the story of the half-baked chickens. Some family stories are best left unheard.

Mealtimes

Breakfast at home was Tang, milk, cereal, toast,
Or Ring Dings—which I loved the most.
Then I'd walk to school with my friend, Ann Marie.

At the ripe age of 12, making lunch fell to Mare—
You were up and awake but in your drinking chair.
An infamous trio: you, the chair, and your mixed drink.

You remember the chair—you were best friends after all—
Spend all day together, then stand up and fall.
I guess it was a four-some—can't forget the floor.

And dinner? Well, it was something that came from a can:
Just heat it and stir it, without burning the pan.
Chop suey, Campbell's soup, tuna, or maybe spam.

On a rare occasion, you gave cooking a try.
"The peas and chicken look fine," I would lie.
Clearly your results equaled the effort you put in.

I didn't want to eat it; it didn't look right,
But you stood there, telling me to take a bite.
I started to cry, and you started "The Blame Game."

You whined that there was only me to eat these "meals."
"There's no appreciation, do you know how that feels?"
And, accepting the blame and guilt, I sat and ate.

This many years later, I finally know
It's the blame and guilt you fed me that I need to outgrow.
Those were far more toxic than any food you made.

My Escape

My escape was school. I loved it! School offered routine and consistency. I knew what to expect each day—there were no surprises. It was an escape from the chaos that could be home.

My Escape

My escape? It was school.
A chance to learn and be me.
It was my refuge. It was safety.

It was a chance to laugh,
To learn to add and subtract,
And I found that I really liked that!

And I learned how to read—
New worlds were at my feet—
I traveled without leaving my seat.

Yes, I'd have to head home
At the end of the day,
Shedding my childhood along the way.

But to all my teachers,
Here's what I want you to know:
You showed me I could change the status quo.

The Gift

Between the ages of five and 20, I remember visiting my favorite great-aunt only about three times, as she lived in Wisconsin. And yet, she was one of the women in my life who had the greatest positive impact on me. It is because of her that I am an avid reader, love to bake, and love gardening. And I believe it is because of the books she gifted me that I did not "lose my way."

The books centered on family, faith, friendship, values, struggles, and successes. These were lessons which I needed to hear and learn as a child, although I don't know how she realized that, living so far away. But I am so thankful for her selection. I re-read them to this day. Most still have their original jackets and are kept in my "Best of the Best" bookcase.

The bookstore where she bought them is still in business, and when my sister and I recently visited Wausau, we stopped in. One of the owners was busy working on the computer, but I intruded on him, because I needed to share the story that the books that helped save me came from his bookstore. He graciously stopped what he was doing to listen to me.

The Gift

My great aunt lived in Wausau.
It's hard to help
When you live that far away.
But, since she loved books,
She made the time
To send some of them my way.

They came from Janke Bookstore—
I know from the
Gold plate on the back cover.
And the books she sent
Helped shape my life,
And made me a book lover.

Little House on the Prairie
And *Little Women*
Were the books she picked for me.
Did she somehow know
That I needed
Examples of love and charity?

I learned kindness is a choice.
That simple acts
Can brighten a person's day.
That just because your
Day wasn't great,
It didn't steal the joy away.

I learned lessons about life
Reading those books—
I wish I could tell her so.
She changed the outcome
Of my life
Sending those books, long ago.

Easter Day

Yes, mom, it's your body, but it's MY life. And it was overcome with confusion, fear, and a sense of being not enough. And it wasn't only my life. Looking at just this one day in the history of your drinking, here is a tally of the number of people's lives impacted:

Your 3 children

12 nieces/nephews

6 brothers/sisters and in-laws

2 ambulance drivers

? and who knows how many medical personnel once you arrived at the hospital.

Easter Day

We came home from Mass
And were faced with a world-class mess throughout the place.
Please, God, not again. We froze, lost in an embrace.

Mare took the first step,
And I just crept behind her. Dried blood on the wall.
Broken glass. Pictures askew. That's what I recall.

You were in a heap.
Comatose? Dead? Asleep? We just stood there in fear,
Called the aunts ... again. Wished we were anywhere but here.

It was Easter Day.
Still, the aunts came right away; even their kids got packed—
Hoping, perhaps, to keep things "Matter of fact."

We were sent outside.
I just wanted to hide. No one knew what to say.
Who expected to be *here* on Easter Day?

There was no chatter.
We had managed to shatter their innocence, too,
Waiting outside for the ambulance for you.

I have no recall
Of what happened to all the mess, the cats, to us.
And till now, this was something I didn't discuss.

Norwich State Hospital

I have no other words.

Norwich State Hospital

Norwich State Hospital.
Back in the day that is where they sent one away
To "dry out." But it never seemed to work for you,
At least, not for more than a month or two.

We visited you there.
But that's a place where there is no space for grace.
Hopelessness, fear, despair, devastation—for sure.
But why send anyone there for a cure?

I remember too much
About that hell. Locked doors, bars, gates—a prison cell.
Deceiving, with its green lawn and the river near.
That first visit, I thought you might be happy there.

But happy's not the word.
You wanted out. We were overwhelmed and looked about
For anyone. We were three kids, in over our head.
I wished I'd stayed home and watched cartoons, instead.

Our visit brought no joy
To you or us. All I wanted to do was rush
Out the door. I didn't think I could take anymore
Of all the heartbreak I witnessed on that floor.

Some people were rocking—
Not in a chair, but squatting on the floor with uncombed hair.
The halls smelled. People yelled, but no one heard.
You couldn't understand them, their speech was slurred.

We left too soon for you
But not nearly soon enough for the three of us.
No one spoke for the hour that it took to drive—
We were too busy just trying to survive.

Decades later, I returned,
Since I had learned it was to be razed and then turned
Into homes, or an entertainment venue or such.
I needed to go back. To see it. To touch

The buildings one last time.
And I knew why. Closure. A chance to clarify
My feelings. I wanted to throw stone after stone—
I wanted those buildings to feel the pain I'd felt of being left
    alone.

The Car Ride

These two poems reflect the feelings and thoughts of a 10-year-old in a time before cell phones, when staying in touch involved memorizing numbers or maintaining an address book. I think my biggest fear about the mention of foster care or an orphanage wasn't the uncertainty of those places, but the realization that I would have no way of getting in touch with my brother or sister to tell them where I was. I did not know where my brother was staying, and I didn't have my aunt's number memorized where my sister was staying. When you are 10, it is terrifying to realize you are utterly alone.

The Car Ride

What terrorized me so, so many years ago,
As you drove me away from all I knew?

The anger in your voice? Or the fact I had no choice
Of where my next home and school would be?

No clue of where I'd sleep? Or if I could keep
My clothes, my toys, my friends? Or was it—

"You could be in foster care, or an orphanage!"
You yelled loud and clear. And I heard the words and the message
  beneath.

But *you* chose to take *me* in, so then why begin
To talk of giving me away on the car ride?

The fear within me grew. I wanted to run from you,
But where do you run when you have no home?

My only world was gone, and you just went on and on
About how lucky I should feel. Would you?

Could you please? Please. Just stop and see
This scared 10-year-old me?
And show some gentleness and mercy ... I am so alone.

My Reflection on the Selection

As an adult, I fully realize how blessed we were to have relatives who cared enough to open their homes and lives to us, and to be willing to disrupt their lives and their children's lives. It was hard enough when it was for several months, but this final time, they were making a commitment for an undetermined amount of time. An amazing gift to all of us. Like me and my siblings, they were forced into a situation they never asked for and there was no guidebook for any of us to follow.

My Reflection on the Selection

I'm trying to see this from your point of view,
To understand how it inconvenienced you.
How frustrated and angry you must have been,
Realizing you had to step up, again.

I get it—you'd already done this before,
And why should you have to do anything more?
I don't think you planned on stepping up that night—
It was time for someone else to "do what's right."

I was around the corner, listening in—
Like picking teams—"Let the selection begin!"
Jim, being 19, he could live with a friend;
Mare to Aunt Mary; but I was a loose end.

The youngest of three, I could be there awhile,
A thought that didn't make anyone smile.
The silence lengthened, I just slid to the floor—
It's crushing to think no one wants you anymore.

"We'll take her," I heard. Then, "Get some stuff, let's go."
What should I pack? What would I need? How could I know?
I grabbed a few things then we were in the car.
"You better realize how lucky you are!"

"You could be in foster care," you barked at me.
"Or an orphanage," and then I saw plainly—
It was duty, not love, that made you say yes
To taking me on with all the added stress.

We finally arrived, but I had no bed.
"You'll sleep with your cousin tonight," you said.
But her bed and her heart had no room for me.
She hadn't asked for extended family.

Did you know I slept on the bedspread, in my clothes,
Because pajamas? I hadn't packed those.
Did you stop and think about all I had lost?
Or were you focused on the burden and cost?

No jammies. No brother. No sister. No mom.
Night one of how many? I had to stay calm.
There was no one to talk to. No one to hold.
Just me, telling myself, "Just do as you're told."

I wish someone had taken a minute to say,
"Welcome! This sure has been a rough day."
Because, I knew I was lucky for a place to be,
But I needed to hear someone say they loved me.

Resilient

Sometimes I think the saying, "Kids are resilient," was created by people who didn't want to take responsibility for the chaos they brought into their children's lives. But I do believe kids *can* be resilient, if they have the loving support of someone to talk to, someone to listen to them, someone who will hear their fears, and help them to navigate through them.

I do not remember anyone ever sitting down with me to tell me about an upcoming move, or about mom going to Norwich State Hospital. People would just show up one day, we'd quickly pack, and we were on our way. As a result, my childhood felt disjointed, as reflected in the disjointedness of "Resilient."

Resilient

They say kids are resilient,
But I think that's a lie.
We just wait till we're alone to cry, as we try

To make sense of our new normal.
A new life that is thrust
Upon us. My heart forms a crust. And how unjust

It is. I did nothing wrong,
And yet nothing feels right
As I try to fall asleep tonight. And fear bites

At me. Terror claws at me.
I heard, "How lucky you are!"
By such an angry uncle driving the car

Away. I'm not resilient,
Here in bed, curled up tight,
Holding in sobs, wishing I was home tonight.

But home no longer exists.
The ambulance took mom.
Not too surprising since the house looked like a bomb

Had gone off. So now I live
Where I am not wanted.
Where my days and nightmares are constantly haunted

By "I wish things were better."
And "I wish I'd been enough
To make mom stop drinking that stuff."

The Brink

I was on the brink for most of my childhood and young adulthood, wondering if I was destined to become my mother—to follow her path. In high school we had a speaker who talked about alcoholism and the percentage of children who follow in the footsteps of alcoholic parents. "You don't have to be the next statistic," she said.

Her words made me realize that I had a choice, that it was not a foregone conclusion. That day, I vowed that I would never get drunk. That I would never become an alcoholic. That I would never put my children through the turmoil and chaos I had lived through.

And so, I lived my life exactly the opposite of what I observed in my mother. It is not the way I wanted to learn—I felt like I was a film negative: the opposite. My love of reading came in handy, because I read everything I could get my hands on about being a good spouse and parent. And when I encountered people who had values or traits I admired, I worked hard to emulate them—to incorporate the positive values into my life and to squeeze out the negative ones I had observed and absorbed growing up.

The Brink

I wonder, as you sit and pour another drink
So you won't have to feel and think
About the chaos that's your life,
If you've noticed your daughter standing on the brink.

As you drink to forget your loneliness and pain,
I am finding ways to explain
Why my friends can't come here to play.
But it's cool. I know there's a façade to maintain.

Mostly what I learn from you is what NOT to do:
Don't feel. Don't laugh. Just get through
The daily grind. The hopelessness.
Don't seek out joy. Don't ask for help. Don't start anew.

I'm on the brink. But I decide to turn around
Because the escape you have found
Is **not** what I choose for me.
I choose to feel. I choose joy. I choose a better legacy.

I Wonder

Maybe everyone wonders, every once in a while, who they would be if their circumstances were different. I wonder if children of alcoholics think about it more often. And, while it is not a preoccupation of mine, there are many days I have wondered, "Who would I be today if I didn't have to grow up that way?"

I Wonder

Sometimes, I wonder who I might be
If you had never started drinking.
I'd like myself more, be self-assured,
At least, that is what I am thinking.

I wouldn't second-guess each action;
I'd be outgoing and quick to smile.
I'd have more friends, maybe more hobbies.
I wouldn't think I'm always on trial.

But the biggest difference in my life
Would be the feelings I'd let myself feel
Since my heart wouldn't have turned to stone.
I think I'd have fewer layers to peel.

Sometimes, I wonder what I'm feeling,
And if it's okay to feel this way.
If you had never started drinking,
Would I be wondering this today?

College

Most days at college I could forget about my family situation or put it on the back-burner. Other times, it was glaringly obvious. Move-in day at college was one. Parents helping with boxes. Moms making beds. Parents and their freshman walking the campus and attending events together. However, as tough as move-in day was, it paled in comparison to the fast-approaching Parents' Weekend.

My roommates had never asked why my mom and dad hadn't moved me in, and I never offered an explanation, not even as Parents' Weekend loomed. When conversations about the weekend surfaced, I would make an excuse and leave the room. I became good friends with the library in the weeks leading up to Parents' Weekend.

College

Arriving at college
With no parents in tow
Was awkward, to say the least.
But nothing compared
To Parents' Weekend
When my anxieties increased.

As my roommates
Anticipated Mom and Dad,
I found ways to disappear.
I wanted to share
In their excitement,
But I felt I had no right to be there.

By Saturday night
They all knew no one had come,
And then invites came my way.
But, I'd never
Be able to repay them,
So said, "Thanks, maybe another day."

I desperately wanted
To say "Yes" and just go;
Pretend we were family.
To peruse a menu,
To chat and to laugh—
Imagine it's where I was meant to be.

Instead, I told myself
"Give them their time alone"—
It seemed the right thing to do.
But later in the day,
Sitting alone in the room,
I wished I'd handled it in a better way.

Decades

As a child of an alcoholic, I spent my childhood thinking and believing that my behaviors could change my mother's ... if only I listened better; if I got better grades; if I did more chores around the house. It led to a lifetime of trying to please my mother and then others. And, when their behaviors didn't change as a result of my behaviors, it led to a lifetime of believing that I am not enough.

Decades

Did you know I spent my childhood
Trying to be perfect and good
In the hopes that you would not pour another drink?

And that I spent my teenage years
Not feeling and not shedding tears?
Hiding behind my fears—not knowing what to think?

My 20s were a lot of fun,
Wondering "What should I have done?"
And so I would just run instead of getting close.

My 30s were not quite as bad—
I could see some blessings I had,
Although my armor-clad heart was comatose.

For every decade that's gone by
I still can't help but wonder why
Nothing that I would try could make you change your ways.

I feel like a failure still,
Because I could not change your will
As our family careened downhill. Not your worries, anyways.

Just keep track of all of your gin.
As for your children? We'll begin
To reverse the tailspin and change the legacy we leave.

The Burden

In witnessing the numerous times so many people's lives were affected by having to accommodate me, care for me, look out for me, I began to see myself as a burden. The weight of being a burden to someone is crushing.

I felt my brother bore the majority of the responsibility in raising me and had to adjust his life accordingly. As an adult with the added benefit of therapy, I realize I did not create the situation that resulted in him having to take on the responsibility of looking after me, but I still struggle with the thoughts of holding him back.

The Burden

Jim, I carry the weight of your stolen childhood on my back
And I lack the ability to forgive myself for taking it from you.

At eleven, you went from being a child to being a man
And I can see you with the weight of the world on your shoulders,
    where it doesn't belong.

Did you hate me for the childhood I had, with you acting as my
    dad?
Were you mad that I had a more carefree life, not shouldering
    the strife around us?

I was too young to see that my expectations added weight,
And I hate that I did not notice sooner; that I became The
    Burden.

I want you to know that I wish you had been free to just be
Who you were meant to be. That your childhood had been
    carefree;
That you did not have to be a dad to me.

I did not know I was casting you in roles you might not desire;
That you might tire of someone tagging after you, asking what
    you were about to do.

I did not know your decisions in life had to account for me.
Where would you be, where would you have flown, if the weight
    you carried had not grounded you?

Receiving

One day my therapist asked me, "How are you at receiving?" "Receiving what?" I replied. In retrospect, I am not sure why I wanted a specific example as I know I am not good at receiving most things. Gifts. Money. Compliments. I feel ... ill at ease? Unworthy?

There is a part of me that believes I need to earn whatever comes my way, that it cannot be freely given to me. So I deflect or reject it, or make a joke to circumvent it. Perhaps part of this is a result of having grown up without positive reinforcement. When receiving, it is difficult to know how to deal with it or how to respond appropriately if you haven't had practice.

Receiving

I was talking to a friend the other day,
I was about to read a reflection I wrote.
She said, "I'm sure it will be a masterpiece,"
And my response stuck in my throat.

I rejected and deflected her compliment,
I hadn't read a word, so how could she know?
I couldn't accept something I hadn't earned,
I knew she meant well, though.

I tried to explain my deflection to her,
And she tried to explain her compliment to me.
She said, "Sometimes you don't have to earn things,
Sometimes you accept them freely."

I wonder if I'll be able to do that,
If I'll ever unlearn and stop deflecting.
I wonder how I would even teach myself.
Can you learn that by reflecting?

As children, when we're given something, we glow
With the excitement and joy that it brings to us.
We don't think, "I didn't earn it, I'm not worthy."
Or, "You should not have made a fuss."

Instead, we bask with delight at being seen,
And know we're deserving of the kindness and love.
Such a priceless time in our journey of life,
When joyfulness fits like a glove.

I'm working at finding that feeling again,
At finding my Self buried beneath all this stuff,
Because then I'll realize I am deserving,
And I'll know that I am enough.

Misconstrued

I did not realize how many non-verbal clues I had picked up and potentially misconstrued during my lifetime. As a child, hearing anger or frustration in someone's voice, it was easy to assume that it was a result of something I had done. I didn't realize that the adult in my life may just be having a bad day and that their frustration may be unrelated to me or my actions.

Now, part of my journey is to discover and let go of the labels I misconstrued.

Misconstrued

Why did I think that I was bad?
Is it because each disagreement I had
With anyone was blamed on me?
That if I spilled something, I was looked at critically?

Or, as a child, did I misconstrue
A look, or tone or some action done by you
That had nothing to do with me?
But saddled me with misbeliefs, anyway, as you can see.

The words "You're bad!" weren't said aloud
But there wasn't a time I felt you were proud
Of me. If nothing positive's said,
It's easy for unspoken messages to be misread.

Somehow, those words that went unsaid
Have managed to take up space inside my head
And have infiltrated my core.
I need to evict them—not let them define me, anymore.

I want to look at me lovingly,
As I am. To realistically look, and see
And determine on my own how I wish to be defined,
And then leave all those other labels behind.

I Realize

Yes, it's your body. But here are just some of the ways that I realize how my life was affected. The one positive in it all is that I was able to break the cycle.

I Realize

I realize I don't ever remember you:
Reading a story to me
Asking me about my day
Or where or with whom I was going to play.

I realize I don't ever remember you:
Teaching me to ride a bike
Taking me for a walk in a park
Or comforting me when I was afraid of the dark.

I realize I don't ever remember you:
Laughing, smiling or telling a joke
Asking me what I would like to do
Or teaching me how to tie my shoe.

I realize I don't ever remember you:
Asking me if I liked school
Asking if my homework was done
Asking me if I had fun.

I realize I don't ever remember you:
Saying "I love you" to me
Tucking me in at night
Or saying, "Sweet dreams, don't let the bedbugs bite."

I realize I don't ever remember you:
Hugging me. Affirming me. Seeing me.
And I think, "That just can't be."
But we both know it is.

And I realize the reason I took such joy in my children
Is that I did for them what you couldn't or wouldn't do for me.
I chose to give them a love-filled legacy.

My Wedding

Therapeutic approaches to grief teach the importance of completing the pain within a relationship. It is a chance to review losses and changes during your life, and to write a completion letter to a person explaining the impact the losses or changes had on you. It is a chance to forgive, to apologize and/or to share emotional statements. It is an amazing process and one I went through for several people in my life, living and dead. These next three poems resulted from a completion letter I wrote to my mom.

My Wedding

My wedding day was still months away, but my worrying had
    already begun.
There was going to be an open bar, which meant I had to find
    someone
To keep an eye on you.

"Finding a baby-sitter for Mom" isn't usually on a bride's to-do
    list—
Heaven knows I didn't want it on mine —but I didn't think you'd
    resist
The temptation to drink.

Turns out, I need not have worried, you died a few months
    before I was wed.
Now, along with the grief I was feeling, guilt was running
    rampant in my head
Because I felt ... relieved.

I wouldn't need a baby-sitter. Didn't need to worry who'd drive
    you back.
I didn't need to watch you like a hawk. I could stop acting like a
    maniac.
I could just be ... a bride.

People tell me they're sorry—heartbroken for me that you will
    miss the Big Day.
Out loud I reply, "Yes, it's so sad." But in my head I hear, "It's
    better this way."
I feel relief. And shame.

It's your body, and I say "It is *my* life," but how do I learn to live
    it?
What do I do with all these conflicting feelings? How do I learn
    to permit
Myself to just be me?

The Letter

Completion letters need to have a closing, since you are completing a conversation. It could be, "Sincerely," "Goodbye," or something similar. An endearment also may be attached, if you are able to do so. I was not.

The Letter

Did you know that 37 years after you died
I wrote you a letter?
It was a chance for me to unfetter myself from
The pain, blame, anger and hate I felt.

The feelings all came pouring out, as I bared my heart.
I could not stop the tears
Any more than I could hold back the fears that I'd become you—
Sad and broken about the cards I'd been dealt.

I wrote of your liquor, hid beneath the kitchen sink;
Of putting you to bed;
Of all the words that you never said, like "I love you."
It was so freeing to write that letter.

Except ...

I discovered something I tried to ignore—
Part of you that **was** me.
A part that couldn't find empathy, for either of us.
And all these years, I'd thought I was better.

But when it comes to this, I am exactly like you,
Though not proud of that fact.
But now you'll see you made an impact. And here it is:
I ended the letter with "Goodbye, Mom" but I could not write
"I love you."

Empathy

For me, therapy has been a journey about many things. One of the most powerful has been learning about my Self. Of learning to accept my Self. Forgive my Self. Be my Self.

And it has been a journey of awareness as I realize that the more I do all of these things for my Self, the easier it becomes to do them for others.

Empathy

Why can't I feel empathy for you?
My heart puts on a suit of armor every time I try to.

What is it that has a hold on me?
There are plenty of people for whom I have shown empathy.

With you, there is none to be found.
Just a hardened heart and plenty of judgment to go around.

I say that I have forgiven you.
But with all this turmoil within me, is that remotely true?

There's a part of me closed off to you—
A part that's hurt, abandoned, confused—kept hidden from your
    view—

Which wants to love you for who you are,
Instead of who I wanted you to be. I'm not there, so far.

I need to acknowledge my feelings. To see
How much hurt and pain still resides deep down inside me.

Tell myself I love me as *I am* today
And not for who I think I should be. Being my Self's okay.

Maybe the armor will fall away
When I feel empathy for my Self. Maybe then I'll convey

My empathy and my love for you—
Just as you are, no strings attached. I know it's what I hope to do.

The Dance

On my wedding day, I asked each of the uncles that I had lived with to dance with me. I wanted to take the opportunity to say thank you, because who knew where I would have been without them.

The angry reaction from one uncle caught me off-guard. On that day, I did what I could to put my hurt, and my anger at being rebuffed, on the back burner. As time went on, though, and I looked at it from a different perspective, I realized how my silence easily could have been misinterpreted as ungratefulness. Hindsight is 20/20. I wish I had had the maturity that day to respond with an explanation so that he knew the sacrifices he made for me were not taken for granted.

The Dance

We dance around so many things.
A dance floor. Fears. A conversation.
I never thought much about that before,
Until I encountered your condemnation.

On my wedding day, I asked you
For a dance. I'd rehearsed what I'd say.
"Thank you, with all my heart," I started out.
Then you spoke, and I felt like a castaway.

"It's about time you said 'Thank you,'"
You chastised. "We did so much for you."
I was caught off-guard by your angry tone,
I could not think of what to say or do.

We danced around the awkwardness
Of those words. I prayed the song would end.
I thanked you for the dance, and quickly left,
Thankful that I had other guests to attend.

But, if I could have a re-do
Of that dance, here's what I would have said,
"My silence wasn't being ungrateful,
I know I was blessed to have a home and bed,

It's just that ... I was only 10,
And I wanted my *own* family.
It wasn't until I became an adult
That I could recognize all that you did for me."

I danced around the guilt I felt—
That I hadn't said "thank you" before.
But, in practicing self-compassion and grace,
I realize I don't need *that* dance anymore.

Fitting In

It feels like I spent a majority of my lifetime trying to fit in—trying to be whomever it was that people seemed to expect me to be. But no matter how many aspects of myself I tried to change, it was never quite right.

And then one day I finally said to myself, "Forget it. I'm done. I can't keep doing this." And I stopped trying to change to fit others' expectations. Like me or don't like me. Invite me or don't invite me. I stopped attending certain events and gatherings when I knew toxic people would be there, or I went and made sure I steered clear of them. I arranged a signal with my husband so that he would know I needed to leave *now*, no questions asked.

Deciding to learn to respect my feelings was one of the best decisions of my life.

Fitting In

Here is what I know:
I tried to fit in.
But then you'd begin to make snide comments.

My butt was too big,
My bust was too small.
No comment at all about my kindness,

Or sense of humor,
Or my baking skills.
Did you get your thrills tearing people down?

Did you see me shrink?
See me get smaller?
Did you feel taller? And more powerful?

I couldn't deduce
The problem was you.
Thought I had to do something to change me.

I've changed so often
Trying to fit in
That I can't begin to discern my Self.

So, I no longer try
To fit in, belong.
It just feels too wrong to keep changing Me.

The Fear Within

Chronologically, I am an adult. And yet, so many of my fears and insecurities still seem rooted in childhood. There are parts of me that are stuck. For instance, my own children are grown and out of the house, yet I still have a fear of becoming my mother, of abandoning my children. It makes no sense.

Perhaps fears are like outfits ... every once in a while I need to take them out and look at them and determine if I need them anymore.

The Fear Within

I have a fear within.
It's not a rational fear,
But knowing that
Doesn't make it magically disappear.

When fear's a companion
From the time you were a child,
It settles in,
Waits, while additional fears are compiled.

While still a child, I learned
That I could tuck fears away—
Not deal with them,
Just tell myself, "Tomorrow's a new day."

But now as an adult
I know the lingering fears
Can limit me,
Overpower me, and my Self disappears.

Some fears protected me—
As I needed them to do.
But now I'm safe,
And I need to let them know their job's through.

I don't need to be scared
Of the same things anymore.
I'm an adult,
Things can't hurt me now, that hurt me before.

Fears may be rational
Or irrational, And yet
I need to see
Them as they are: feelings, and not a threat.

You're Fine

I spent most of my life stuffing my feelings down and ignoring them. Partly because, when I was young, there was no one around to share them with. And, as I got older, I thought, "It's in the past. What does it matter? It's over with." So I just kept telling myself, "You're fine. Move on." And it worked ... until it didn't.

You're Fine

Looking back, I'm amazed how often I've told myself "You're
    fine."
Turmoil is raging within me, but I am determined to undermine
What my feelings are trying to convey—
Choosing instead to ignore them; hope they go away.

When that technique hasn't worked, I've chosen to sleep instead.
There is something calming about snuggling under the covers in
    my bed
With complete darkness enveloping me.
A sense of security, though it's temporary.

Often, I want to go back to my old ways of handling things:
Compartmentalizing; Avoiding; Tucking stuff away. Then the
    stings
Disappear, at least for the time being.
But that doesn't do much for my long-term well-being.

At times, I've tried to determine what's wrong, why I feel so
    wired.
I look back at the day to find the cause and settle on, "I'm just
    overtired
Or overwhelmed. I've scheduled too much stuff.
I need a better grasp of when enough is enough."

But there are days I just cannot identify the feeling.
And the inner storms make it appear as if the walls and ceiling
Are closing in on me, hemming me in.
Why can't I identify what I am feeling within?

I wish emotions would come equipped with an instruction book.
Something to show the best way to approach a feeling and look
At it and respond, rather than react;
Address things head-on, rather than being sidetracked.

I think those times I've told myself "You're fine" when I'm not
Is what has me caught in this dilemma. Why I am fraught
With indecision about what's within me;
Why I cannot seem to find my identity.

Redesign

I internalized so many unspoken messages in my lifetime. Someone may not have called me "bad," but their attitudes and/or actions toward me led me to believe they were thinking along those lines. And so I inherited that label.

Now I at least know that I do not have to accept them. I have the option to define, design, and redesign my Self.

Redesign

I know I can't change the past
But why does the hurt last
So far into the future?

Crying brings me some relief
From these emotions called grief,
But it's not a solution.

So I'm reading a grief book
And taking a long look
At my attitudes and Self.

I've found wisdom in the lines
Which may help me redesign
How I approach memories.

I can change how I react
To alter the impact
That the past holds over me.

Stop listening to clichés
And find ways to rephrase
The message I send my Self.

I think it will take a while
For me to learn this new style,
But it will be worth the journey.

Being a Mom

I heard once that we give our children the things we think they need or want, and that many times those equate to what we needed or wanted when we were children. And that what we should do is teach our children to *ask* for what they need or want, once they are able to do that.

When I wrote this poem, I recognized the truth in the first part of the statement. I can so clearly see that all of the things my mom never did for me, all of the things that I needed or wanted her to do for me, are indeed the things that I made sure to do for my children.

As for the second part of the statement? Although my children were already fully grown when I learned this, I let them know that if there was something they wanted or needed from me, to let me know. I am listening.

Being a Mom

To prepare for each birth I read book after book,
But nothing could prepare me for their first look.
Suddenly, I was in love for all I was worth.

I had problems nursing, and many sleepless nights,
But knew they'd end, so before turning out lights
I would just keep telling myself, "You can do this."

And I did do it. I loved them with all my heart.
I read, sang, baked; and I rocked them from the start.
I listened, watched, guarded; and taught them their prayers.

We laughed. We adventured. Saw a movie or two.
We double-dutched until the school bus came through.
There were bubbles, cards, games; and camping out, too.

I went to recitals, open houses, and games.
Had friends over to play, and I learned all their names.
We built a fort, so they'd have a space of their own.

With pride, I watched them grow both inside and out.
With concern, saw them encounter heartbreak, doubt.
And worried as they discerned what the world's about.

I taught them the things I thought they should know,
I taught them they had wings when it was okay to go.
Taught them trust and honesty, kindness and faith.

Of the many gifts that God has given to me
Being a mom is the best, because I can see
That being a mom is the best version of me.

The Assignment

At some point during therapy, it was suggested I write a completion letter to myself. I was unsure of the parameters and so sent a couple of emails back and forth as I tried to understand the purpose, end goal etc. of the letter. In truth, having written about five completion letters to that point, I had a fairly good idea of what I needed to do ... but I was not sure if I was able or willing to accomplish the task. It was a big ask.

In trying to discern my procrastination, I wrote "The Assignment." Writing the poem revealed my fears, which freed up space for me to be able to write the completion letter to my Self. The Managers, Firefighters, and Exiles mentioned in the poem belong to the Internal Family Systems (IFS) methodology. If, like me, you have ever said something like, "There is a part of me that wants to go do that, but there's another part that wants to do this," then you will likely embrace the concepts of IFS.

The Assignment

I need to write a completion letter
And it needs to be addressed to Me.
I need to "unblend"; to get to my "Self,"
But I'm terrified of finding out who I might be.

You're asking me to take away layers
That I have worked decades to erect;
To put aside the Managers and the
Firefighters, and all the Exiles that I can detect.

You're asking me to let down my guard,
To discover what lies at my core.
But in being a burden to others
I was taught to never ask, or wish, or self-explore.

How will I know when I get to my Self?
How will I know when I'm done peeling?
How will I learn it's okay to be me?
And that it's okay to be feeling what I'm feeling?

How Will I Learn?

As an adult child of an alcoholic, I have spent so much time trying to please others, trying to be who they expected or wanted or needed me to be, that I felt clueless as to how to even begin the process of learning what I expected or wanted or needed from myself.

How Will I Learn?

How will I learn it's okay to be me
When I hear a cacophony of voices
Always limiting my choices?

How will I learn it's okay to wish,
And that I'm free to accomplish my desires,
Rather than putting out more fires?

How can I discover what's at my core
When I don't listen anymore to my Self—
My feelings, ignored, on a shelf?

How can I wish or dare to even ask
For someone to notice or bask over me,
When I've been living so silently?

My Voice

In "The Assignment" there is a line that states "I was taught to never ask, or wish, or self-explore." I think this is typical of children of alcoholics. We may start off asking, wishing, self-exploring, but when the answer is always "no," or when the question isn't being heard or received, we learn to stop asking and wishing. And, being in survival mode from day-to-day, there is little, if any, time for self-exploration. Even when we are physically distanced from the alcoholic for years, we don't seem to get our voice back.

My Voice

Somewhere along the way
I lost my voice.
Or perhaps I made a choice
Not to use it.

I think I know which one,
But can't admit
That I made a choice to quit
Speaking my truth.

That's a lot of power
I gave away—
To no longer have a say
About my life.

What was I afraid of,
Not speaking out?
Or did I not think about
Repercussions?

Did I truly not know
All that I'd lose?
Self-respect, the chance to choose,
And to be heard.

I don't know if you'll listen.
Or if you'll care.
But I'll never know, if I share
Only Silence.

What am I afraid of?
Not being heard.
So I'm giving you my word:
My silence ends now.

There Are Days

In my lifetime a recurring theme is the frustration of wondering whether I think and act a certain way because I am an adult child of an alcoholic, or if everyone deals with all of these questions and uncertainty.

There Are Days

There are days I wonder why
I can't just ask for what I want or need,
Then I realize it was you who planted this seed,
This necessity to live life silently.

There are days I wonder why
I stopped dreaming and wishing on a star.
"Dreaming's a waste," you implied. So I sealed them in a jar.
And, regretfully, I never set them free.

There are days I wonder why
I don't know who my Self is anymore.
At what point did I no longer want to explore
The core within, the child who is me?

There are days I wonder why,
If it is your body, it affects me.
Why I have issues asking, dreaming, seeing clearly.
Why, as an adult, I still cannot break free.

Lesson at the Lake

In reminiscing about our childhood one day, my sister and I decided to take an actual trip down Memory Lane. We made a 3,200-mile loop and visited her birthplace, as well as the birthplaces of our dad and our brother. We visited the institution where Dad had been, the towns where our great-aunt and our grandmother had lived, and the cemeteries, too. While listening to her stories, some of the "blanks" in my childhood were filled-in a bit. We shared laughter and tears throughout the journey.

In planning the trip, and seeing our proximity to the Great Lakes, we also made it a goal to put our feet into all five Great Lakes. Our first stop was Lake Ontario. We wanted a picture and, as there was only one other person there, I intruded upon her. She graciously stopped what she was doing in order to take the picture. Her openness to our intrusion was a lesson for me, which I tried to capture in this poem.

Lesson at the Lake
Lake Ontario, 5/21/24

My sister and I arrived at the Lake
And tried to figure out how to take a selfie—
A challenge for her and me!

We saw a young lady on a boulder
And thought that since we were older, she'd understand.
I meandered through the sand.

I apologized for the intrusion—
I could tell she was in seclusion purposefully.
"No worries, it's fine with me.

Alone-time's great, but people-time is too,
So yes, I'll take a picture of you," she stated.
I was impressed and elated.

She got off the rock and reached for my phone.
Then she told us about her milestone—clean eight years.
With courage, she'd faced her fears.

Her name was Sophie, which I won't forget
Since she was so gracious when she let us intrude
On her peace and solitude.

She taught me intrusions could be a gift.
A thought which inspired me to shift, to survey,
My habit of turning away.

Thank you, Sophie, for helping me to see
How wonderful intrusions can be. Who would have guessed
That interruptions could be so blessed?

Letting Go

We don't get a re-do. Sometimes I wish we did. And I don't know if thinking about the "difficult times" is a way to work through them and resolve them, or if it is just a way to stir up the pain and hurt. Or perhaps it is both. But I have realized that while I can't rewrite the past, I can forgive. Forgive others. Forgive my Self. For me, it feels like a step in the right direction.

Letting Go

It's time for me to let go:
Of the guilt, the hurt, the blame.
I've carried them for too long,
Packaged with silence and shame.

I am not letting go of you—
Of the memories we've made—
Of the good times we've shared,
Like all the card games we've played.

But I have finally learned that
I'm responsible for me,
You're responsible for you.
So I'm letting go of "If Only."

I'm letting go of my "What-ifs,"
Letting go of "It's my fault,"
Letting go of the regrets,
Because my heart's become a vault.

It's time to open it, to breathe.
To forgive myself and you.
To stop reliving the past,
Because we don't get a "re-do."

Maybe we could have done better.
Maybe we both did our best.
For certain we were human,
With all of our imperfectness.

It's time for me to let go now,
But I'm not letting go of you.
Just opening up my heart,
It's time to breathe and start anew.

Who I Am

For me, one of the best outcomes of therapy has been the journey of learning to love and accept myself. I used to hate the parts of me that got jealous, or defensive; the parts that couldn't just let things "roll off my shoulders." I was always trying to change, to become different, better. Now, I am able to recognize those parts of me as my "internal system" and I am able to acknowledge the part they played in protecting me throughout my life. They are a loved part of me today. After a year of expert guidance, and with honest, difficult, sometimes heart-breaking introspection on my part, I can look at myself, my strengths and weaknesses, and begin to recognize Who I Am.

Who I Am

I'm sitting at my desk with thoughts swirling in my mind.
I'm contemplating who I am and wonder what I will find
As I think about me.
Do I know my Self completely?

I am strong, because when my mother was weak our family fell
    apart.
I don't want to be strong all the time, but I needed to impart
Strength as a trait—
Something for my children to emulate.

I am witty and have a sense of humor, too. They helped me get
    through.
Sometimes that makes it hard to share my hurt. Who knew
How difficult it could be,
To release humor and discuss the hurt freely?

I am empathetic and kind to some, but hard-hearted to another.
I want to show compassion, but I'm selective, like with my
    mother.
And it doesn't feel like that's okay.
Will it change one day?

I am a rule-lover because as a child, chaos reigned my life.
Sometimes I want to unclench, be free, and learn to just "Be,"
But having no boundaries
Leaves me feeling ill-at-ease.

I am a giver of gifts and kind words since as a child, both were
    rare,
And it left me wondering if someone would care
If I was there or not.
And I don't want someone else to be in that spot.

I am afraid. Afraid that I am not enough. Afraid that I don't meet
Expectations—though I don't know whose. So how can I
    compete
In a race
That doesn't have a face?

I am fiercely protective of so many things: my home, my family,
    my heart.
Since I rarely felt protected or valued, I worked hard to impart
A sense of calmness and peace—
A space of safety and release.

I am an island, since as a child I was often on my own,
Being left to my own devices is all I've ever known,
So I don't even think to ask
For someone to help me with a task.

I am honest because I'm an adult child of an alcoholic and heard
    too many lies,
I chose not to follow that path. I chose not to compromise
The value of truth.
I learned that early on in my youth.

I am a storyteller because stories are a way to validate and affirm
A person's Self. It is the way I choose to emphasize and confirm
That someone is a treasure,
And that I love them beyond measure.

I am courageous, especially when I make the time to learn about
    me,
To love and forgive my Self—despite my faults—and to do it
    compassionately
And often,
So that my heart continues to soften.

I am a baker, reader and gardener, as my namesake before me,
Who shared her love of all of those things so generously.
I am honored to share her name;
To credit her some for the woman I became.

I am bits and pieces of a lifetime that is mainly behind me,
Of relationships and events that have shaped and molded me,
   sometimes splendidly,
Sometimes less.
But I'm learning to be grateful for the journey—the beauty and
   the mess.
Because that is what made me, me.

Epilogue

When I mentioned I was writing a book, someone asked me, "Why? What are your goals?" My initial thought was, "Does a book have to have a goal? Can't you just write a book as a form of self-expression?" But since the question kept coming forward in my mind, I gave it some thought and realized I did have some goals.

First, to give words to some of the feelings that I was feeling and experiences that I had and that you may be dealing with in your life. I know the positive impact *Up a Road Slowly* had on me when some of my feelings were finally identified, so perhaps this book will do the same for you.

Second, to share the message that you don't have to be a statistic. Hearing that message was life-changing for me, so I want to keep passing it along. It is *your* life. And while so much of what we think or how we react may be due to our upbringing, we can make a different choice. We can choose a different path. We can break the cycle.

Third, don't ever be afraid to ask for help. Find a therapist or someone that you trust, who provides a space of safety and security. Don't be afraid to keep looking if you don't find it right away. As an adult child of an alcoholic, I have an "I can do it on my own," mentality, because for years I had to do things on my own. But there are amazing therapists out there, and you do not have to make this journey alone. Sometimes having someone by your side makes all the difference.

Fourth, after writing "The Letter," my goal was to reach a point of forgiveness, understanding, grace ... or whatever it was that

I needed to be able to write "P.S. Mom, I love you," at the end of this book. I have not achieved that goal. I made a decision to forgive my mom, but forgiveness is sometimes a process for me, and not an instantaneous outcome. A work in progress, so to speak. I do know I can say that I honored my mom. When she was in the assisted living facility, my sister and I picked her up every Saturday and went bowling, or shopping, or whatever, and then took her out to lunch. On Sunday, my brother and sister-in-law and I would have Mom over for cards or games and dinner. It was a priority to us, and we kept faithful to it.

Is honoring someone a form of loving them? I don't know. I think I loved her the best that I was able to love her, but perhaps not as much as she deserved. I did not live her life. I don't know and can only imagine what it must have been like to be young, have three young children, and have the husband she adored suddenly take ill and have her entire world pulled from beneath her feet.

So, for now, I will write, "P.S. Mom, I loved you to the best of my ability." Perhaps, as I continue this journey of self-compassion and grace, I will reach my goal.

I wish you a journey filled with discovery, joy, and compassion.

References

Alcott, L. M. (1868). *Little Women*. Roberts Brothers.

Hunt, Irene. (1966). *Up a Road Slowly*. Follett.

Schwartz, R. C., & Sweezy, M. (2019). *Internal Family Systems Therapy*. The Guilford Press.

Wilder, L. I. (1935–1943). *The Little House Series*. Harper & Brothers.

About the Author

L. Harrington has enjoyed writing humorous, light-hearted poetry since adolescence. Break a toe on a doorstop? A poem will be written within the hour. Turning 50? An "Ode to 50" will appear in your next birthday card. But heart-searching poetry? Not until the death of her brother brought her to therapy and a journey through the grief of his loss, and then the journey through the grief of being an adult child of an alcoholic.

L. Harrington lives in Connecticut with her husband. They have two adult children. She loves baking, gardening, reading, photography, and kayaking the quiet waters of Connecticut.

This is her first published work.

To contact the author, you may email her at:

LHarringtonAuthor@gmail.com